REMARKABLE PEOPLE

Hillary Clinton

by Tom Riddolls and Judy Wearing

Published by Weigl Publishers Inc.
350 5th Avenue, Suite 3304, PMB 6G
New York, NY 10118-0069

Website: www.weigl.com

Library of Congress Cataloging-in-Publication Data

Riddolls, Tom.
 Hillary Clinton / Tom Riddolls and Judy Wearing.
     p. cm. -- (Remarkable people)
 Includes index.
 ISBN 978-1-60596-620-5 (hard cover : alk. paper) -- ISBN 978-1-60596-621-2 (soft
cover : alk. paper)
1. Clinton, Hillary Rodham--Juvenile literature. 2. Presidents' spouses--United
States--Biography--Juvenile literature. 3. Legislators--United States--Biography--
Juvenile literature. 4. Women legislators--United States--Biography--Juvenile
literature. 5. United States. Congress. Senate--Biography--Juvenile literature. 6.
 Presidential candidates--United States--Biography--Juvenile literature. I. Wearing,
Judy. II. Title.
 E997.C55R54 2009
 973.929092--dc22
 [B]
                                    2009007807

Printed in China
1 2 3 4 5 6 7 8 9 0 13 12 11 10 09

Editor: Nick Winnick
Design: Terry Paulhus

Photograph Credits
Weigl acknowledges Getty Images as the primary image supplier for this title.
Unless otherwise noted, all images herein were obtained from Getty Images and
its contributors.

Every reasonable effort has been made to trace ownership and to obtain
permission to reprint copyright material. The publishers would be pleased
to have any errors or omissions brought to their attention so that they may
be corrected in subsequent printings.

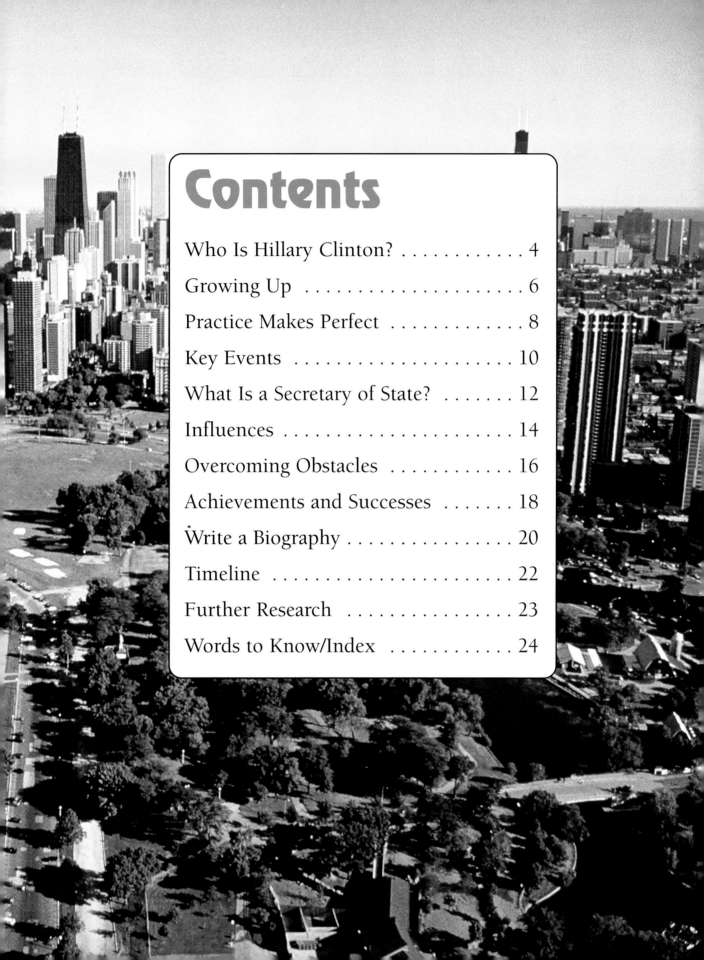

Contents

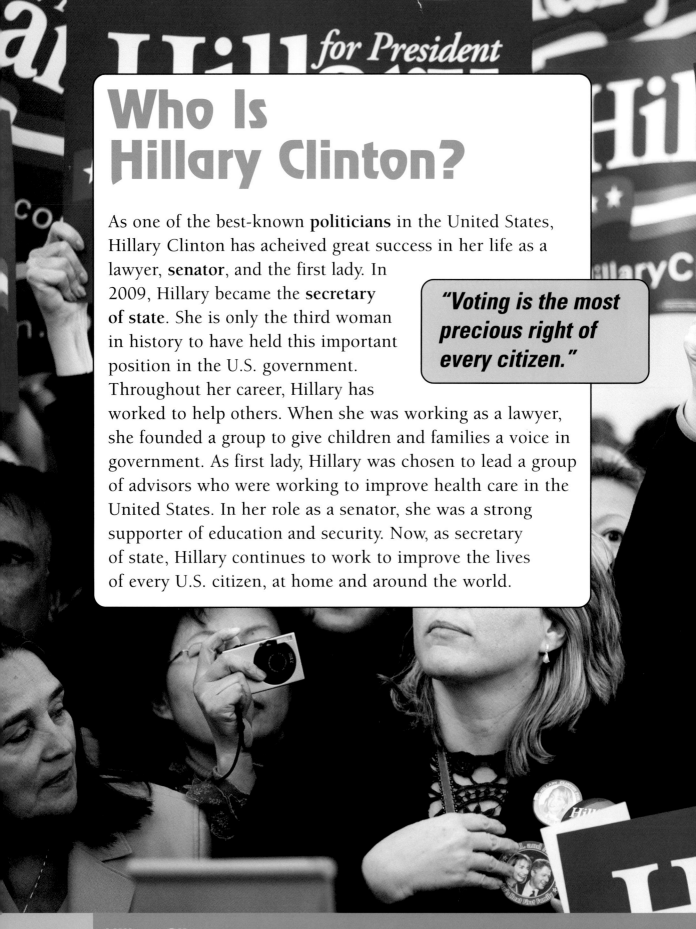

Who Is Hillary Clinton?

As one of the best-known **politicians** in the United States, Hillary Clinton has acheived great success in her life as a lawyer, **senator**, and the first lady. In 2009, Hillary became the **secretary of state**. She is only the third woman in history to have held this important position in the U.S. government. Throughout her career, Hillary has worked to help others. When she was working as a lawyer, she founded a group to give children and families a voice in government. As first lady, Hillary was chosen to lead a group of advisors who were working to improve health care in the United States. In her role as a senator, she was a strong supporter of education and security. Now, as secretary of state, Hillary continues to work to improve the lives of every U.S. citizen, at home and around the world.

"Voting is the most precious right of every citizen."

Growing Up

Hillary Diane Rodham was born in Chicago, Illinois, on October 26, 1947, to Hugh Ellsworth Rodham and Dorothy Emma Howell. Hugh was a successful businessman in the clothing industry. In 1950, the couple had a second child, who they named Hugh after his father. Their third child, Anthony, was born in 1954.

Hillary's parents encouraged their children to reach their full potential. Hillary worked hard in school, and she often had straight "A"s on her report card. She dreamed of being an astronaut and often pretended to make trips to the Moon.

Hillary's family were members of the **Republican** party. As she grew up, Hillary began to have different political views from those of her family. As a teenager, she spent a great deal of time volunteering to help others in less-fortunate parts of Chicago.

■ As a child, Hillary lived in the Park Ridge suburb of Chicago.

Get to Know Illinois

WISCONSIN
IOWA
ILLINOIS
INDIANA
MISSOURI
KENTUCKY

0 — 100 Miles
0 — 100 Kilometers

ANIMAL
White-tailed deer

FLAG

BIRD
Cardinal

More than 12 million people live in Illinois. This makes it the fifth-largest state in terms of population.

Chicago's main airport, O'Hare, is the second-busiest airport in the world.

The first skyscraper in the United States was built in Chicago in 1885.

Illinois became a state on December 3, 1818.

Chicago's coldest temperature was –27°F (–33°C), recorded in 1985. Powerful wind that day made it feel like –83°F (–64°C).

Think about it!

Two of the nation's most important politicians today, Hillary Clinton and Barack Obama, have lived in Chicago. Research the politics of this city. How do you think living here affected the political beliefs of these two leaders? Now, research the politics in your area. How do they affect your own beliefs and your daily life?

Practice Makes Perfect

Hillary's involvement in politics began when she was a teenager. In 1964, Republican Barry Goldwater ran for president. Goldwater was an outspoken politician, and many young people liked the ideas he had for the country. Hillary, her best friend, and many other teenage girls volunteered to help the Goldwater campaign. They were called the "Goldwater Girls."

After high school, Hillary attended Wellesley College, a private school known for its high quality. When she graduated from Wellesley, Hillary was chosen to give the commencement address to her class. She was the first student to be given this honor. Hillary's speech at Wellesley College brought her a great deal of attention. She criticized Senator Edward Brooke, who had just addressed the class.

■ Barry Goldwater lost the 1964 election to Democrat Lyndon B. Johnson.

When she finished speaking, the crowd gave her a standing ovation that lasted seven minutes. *Life* magazine wrote an article about the event, spreading Hillary's name across the United States.

After graduating from Wellesley College, Hillary entered law school at Yale, one of the most respected schools in the United States for its law, medicine, and science departments. While there, Hillary met her future husband, Bill Clinton. In 1973, Hillary graduated from Yale with a degree in law and began her professional career. The following year, Hillary moved to Arkansas to teach law at the University of Arkansas. Bill also taught at the university. The two wed in 1975. Their only child, Chelsea, was born in 1980.

■ Hillary has said that, when she was young, she was Republican in her mind, but Democratic at heart.

Key Events

Hillary became the first lady of Arkansas when Bill was elected governor in 1979. As the first lady, Hillary created the Arkansas Advocates for Children and Families. This group was created to bring the needs of low-income families to the state government. In 1979, Hillary became the first female **partner** at Rose Law Firm. She continued to work there until 1992.

The Clinton family moved to the White House when Bill became president in 1993. Bill chose Hillary to lead the team that would find ways to improve health care in the United States.

Hillary ran for a seat in the **Senate** in 2000. She won, becoming the first woman to hold a Senate seat in New York, and the only first lady to hold elected office.

In 2008, Hillary ran for the Democratic party's **nomination** for president. After a close race, Barack Obama won the nomination. When Barack became president, he chose Hillary to be secretary of state.

■ Bill and Hillary moved to Chappaqua, New York, in 1999.

Thoughts from Hillary

As a politician, Hillary often speaks to the public. It is important for politicians to speak, and respond, to citizens. In this way, politicians can learn what people believe to be important and defend those beliefs.

Hillary remembers learning that, at one time, only men were allowed to be astronauts.

"To have my government tell me that there was something I couldn't do because I was a girl was shocking to me."

Hillary talks about priorities.
"We must stop thinking of the individual and start thinking about what is best for society."

Hillary believes the government should help people.

"No government can love a child, and no policy can substitute for a family's care. But at the same time, government can either support or undermine families."

Hillary has strong values and beliefs.

"I have gone from a Barry Goldwater Republican to a new Democrat, but I think my underlying values have remained pretty constant: individual responsibility and community."

Hillary knows the importance of debate in politics.

"I'm sick and tired of people who say that if you debate and disagree with this administration, somehow you're not patriotic. We need to stand up and say we're Americans, and we have the right to debate and disagree."

Hillary works hard to keep her life balanced.

"Our lives are a mixture of different roles. Most of us are doing the best we can to find whatever the right balance is... For me, that balance is family, work, and service."

What Is a Secretary of State?

The president chooses a secretary of state to be in charge of the United States Department of State. The **State Department** is responsible for dealing with other nations. It protects U.S. citizens when they travel to other countries and helps U.S. businesses compete in the world market.

The State Department tells the public about the United States' dealings with other countries and gives feedback to the government. The secretary of state is responsible for keeping the president informed about how the United States interacts with other countries.

When a secretary of state is chosen by the president, this person is presented to the senate. The senate can then decide to accept or reject the president's choice. When Hillary was chosen as secretary of state, 94 senators agreed with the decision. Only two disagreed with her appointment.

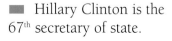 Hillary Clinton is the 67th secretary of state.

Secretaries of State 101

Thomas Jefferson (1743–1826)

Thomas Jefferson was one of the **Founding Fathers** of the United States. He was the main writer of the Declaration of Independence. Jefferson served as the country's first secretary of state, the second vice president, and the third president of the United States. He was well known as a **scholar** and a **diplomat**, and had many skills outside of politics. Among these talents were **architecture**, inventing, and the study of plants.

Madeleine Albright (1937–)

Madeline Albright was selected by President Bill Clinton to be the 64th secretary of state. She was the first woman to serve in that position. Earlier, she had been the United States' ambassador to the United Nations. She has worked for peace and stability in eastern Europe, both as UN ambassador and after her term as secretary of state. She is currently a professor of diplomacy at Georgetown University.

Colin Powell (1937–)

Colin Powell was selected by President George W. Bush to be the 65th secretary of state. Before taking this position, Powell had a long and successful military career. He had been a four-star general and was given many awards for his service, including the Purple Heart and Bronze Star. Powell served as National Security Advisor to President Ronald Reagan, and Chairman of the Joint Chiefs of Staff. He was the first African American secretary of state.

Condoleezza Rice (1954–)

Condoleezza Rice was chosen by President George W. Bush to be secretary of state during his second term of office. During Bush's first term, she served as National Security Advisor. Earlier in her career, Rice was a professor of political science at Stanford University. She advised President George H.W. Bush about the fall of the **Soviet Union** in the late 1980s and early 1990s. She has been a strong supporter of Middle East peace and finding diplomatic solutions to problems. Rice is a skilled piano player, and has played with the Denver Symphony and cellist Yo Yo Ma. She was the first African American woman to be secretary of state.

American Political Parties

There are two main political parties in the United States. They are called the Democratic Party and the Republican party. People vote for leaders that belong to one of these two parties. The Democratic Party's view is that the rights of individuals are most important in a successful country. The Republican Party's view is that business and the **economy** are key factors in the United States' success.

Influences

As a young girl, Hillary was active in her community. When she was not in school, she went to bible study groups and helped her fellow Chicagoans. When Hillary turned 13, Donald G. Jones became the new minister at her church. Donald and Hillary traveled to Chicago's inner city so that she could see how less fortunate children lived. Donald encouraged Hillary to read about people who worked to improve living conditions for all citizens. Soon, she was volunteering to watch children for working parents who could not afford caregivers.

Hillary was at a Chicago event when civil rights leader Martin Luther King, Jr. spoke about human rights. He believed that all people should be treated equally. Listening to King inspired Hillary throughout her life.

■ Martin Luther King, Jr. was an important figure during the Civil Rights movement of the 1950s and 1960s. King worked hard to establish freedom for all people. He believed that everyone deserved fair and equal treatment. King's powerful speeches brought hope to people all over the world.

While Hillary was in university, a professor named Marian Wright Edelman became one of her mentors. Edelman was the first African American woman to become a lawyer in Mississippi. She was a strong supporter of children's rights, and created the Children's Defense Fund. Edelman pushed the U.S. government to improve adoption programs and child care funding. Hillary learned a great deal about protecting people's rights from Edelman.

THE CLINTON FAMILY

Hillary married Bill Clinton in 1975. Like Hillary, Bill was a lawyer and politician. Shortly after they married, Bill became the governor of Arkansas, making Hillary Arkansas's first lady. Together, Bill and Hillary worked for better education and health care. The couple's only child, Chelsea, was born in 1980. Chelsea helped her mother in 2008 when she ran for the Democratic Party's nomination.

■ During Hillary's campaign for the Democratic nomination for president, Chelsea visited more than 100 colleges and universities to speak with students in an effort to gain their support for her mother.

Overcoming Obstacles

Hillary grew up in a time when women were not allowed to work in certain jobs. When Hillary was 14, she wrote a letter to NASA asking how a young woman could become an astronaut. A representative wrote back and explained that only men could travel into space. This upset Hillary. She decided not to let this obstacle stand in her way of being successful.

Throughout her career, Hillary has had to deal with the idea that women could not do the same jobs as men. Even during the 2008 race for the Democratic nomination, the media often made comments about her gender. Hillary wanted people decide to vote for her based on her ideas, not her gender.

■ Hillary encourages children to work hard to achieve their dreams.

Hillary has spent a great deal of her career in the public eye. Much of what she says is recorded, printed, and broadcast. This means that she must always be careful about her choice of words and her actions. As a well-known politician, her decisions are often talked about by people around the world.

Hillary knows that it is difficult to make every citizen happy when making a political decision. She must deal with criticism from people who feel she has made a poor decision. Sometimes, people even poke fun at her by drawing cartoons or **impersonating** her on comedy shows. Hillary has learned to respond to such acts in a positive way and ignore stories that are untrue.

People with cameras often follow Hillary, trying to take her picture.

Achievements and Successes

Hillary has always wanted to make people's lives better. In college, she was voted Most Likely to Become President. Since then, Hillary has won many awards that celebrate her work.

In 1973, Hillary published an article called "Children Under the Law" in the *Harvard Educational Review*. The article talked about children's rights and became a common source of information for teachers. Hillary's legal work had her named one of the 100 most influential lawyers in America in 1988 and 1991 by the *National Law Journal*.

Hillary is also an author. In 1996, she wrote *It Takes A Village: And Other Lessons Children Teach Us*, a book about the role of society in raising children.

■ Hillary often takes time to meet her supporters and sign copies of her book.

The following year, Hillary won a Grammy award for Best Spoken Word Album, for the audio book of *It Takes A Village*. In 2003, Hillary released *Living History*, a book about her life. It became a *New York Times* Best Seller as soon as it was released.

Along with Senators Ted Kennedy and Orin Hatch, Hillary created the State Children's Health Insurance Plan in 1997. This program was formed to help low-income families with large bills for their children's health care. Hillary also was key to the creation of Vital Voices, a group that teaches business skills to women and promotes women's participation in government around the world.

ARKANSAS ADVOCATES FOR CHILDREN AND FAMILIES

Created by Hillary Clinton in 1977, Arkansas Advocates for Children and Families provides a voice in the Arkansas state government for women, children, and less-fortunate families. The members of Arkansas Advocates for Children and Families (AACF) are lawyers and students who believe that all people should have a say in how government affects their lives. The AACF educates the public and the state about issues that can affect lower-income families and children. This organization works to remind the government to create laws that respect the rights of all people. **www.aradvocates.org**

Write a Biography

A person's life story can be the subject of a book. This kind of book is called a biography. Biographies describe the lives of remarkable people, such as those who have achieved great success or have done important things to help others. These people may be alive today, or they may have lived many years ago. Reading a biography can help you learn more about a remarkable person.

At school, you might be asked to write a biography. First, decide who you want to write about. You can choose a politician, such as Hillary Clinton, or any other person you find interesting. Then, find out if your library has any books about this person. Learn as much as you can about him or her. Write down the key events in this person's life. What was this person's childhood like? What has he or she accomplished? What are his or her goals? What makes this person special or unusual?

A concept web is a useful research tool. Read the questions in the following concept web. Answer the questions in your notebook. Your answers will help you write your biography review.

- Where does this individual currently reside?
- Does he or she have a family?

- What did you learn from the books you read in your research?
- Would you suggest these books to others?
- Was anything missing from these books?

- Where and when was this person born?
- Describe his or her parents, siblings, and friends.
- Did this person grow up in unusual circumstances?

Your Opinion

Adulthood

Childhood

WRITING A BIOGRAPHY

Main Accomplishments

Help and Obstacles

Work and Preparation

- What is this person's life's work?
- Has he or she received awards or recognition for accomplishments?
- How have this person's accomplishments served others?

- What was this person's education?
- What was his or her work experience?
- How does this person work; what is or was the process he or she uses or used?

- Did this individual have a positive attitude?
- Did he or she receive help from others?
- Did this person have a mentor?
- Did this person face any hardships?
- If so, how were the hardships overcome?

Timeline

YEAR	HILLARY CLINTON	WORLD EVENTS
1947	Hillary Diane Rodham is born on October 26.	Sessions of the U.S. Congress are shown on television for the first time.
1962	Hillary goes to Chicago and hears Martin Luther King, Jr. speak.	John Glenn becomes the first American astronaut to **orbit** Earth.
1969	Hillary gives a speech to university students. *Life* magazine writes a story about it.	The United States begins to bring soldiers home from the Vietnam War.
1975	Hillary marries Bill Clinton.	South Vietnam surrenders, ending the Vietnam War.
1993	Hillary becomes first lady of the United States.	Nelson Mandela, president of South Africa, wins the **Nobel Peace Prize.**
2001	Hillary becomes a senator for New York.	The United States and its allies invade Afghanistan to find the people responsible for the terrorist attack on New York earlier that year.
2009	Hillary becomes secretary of state.	Barack Obama becomes president of the United States.

Further Research

How can I find out more about Hillary Clinton?

Most libraries have computers that connect to a database that contains information on books and articles about different subjects. You can input a key word and find material on the person, place, or thing you want to learn more about. The computer will provide you with a list of books in the library that contain information on the subject you searched for. Non-fiction books are arranged numerically, using their call number. Fiction books are organized alphabetically by the author's last name.

Websites

Hillary Clinton official website
www.hillaryclinton.com

To learn more about the State Department, visit
www.state.gov/aboutstatedepartment

Words to Know

architecture: the art of designing buildings

diplomat: a person who helps groups with different interests reach compromises

economy: the money and business of a country

founding fathers: men responsible for the creation of the United States

impersonating: using make-up and acting to take on the appearance of another person

Nobel Peace Prize: an award given every year to someone who fights for peace and makes a difference

nomination: deciding which politician will represent a party in the race for president

orbit: to travel around a planet

partner: a person who assumes part of the risk and part of the profit in a business

politicians: people who represent citizens of their area in government

republican: politicians who feel that personal freedom and the economy are most important

scholar: a specialist in a certain area of study

secretary of state: the head of the U. S. Department of State

senate: a group of elected politicians who make decisions about how to best run the country

senator: a politician chosen by the people of a state to represent them in the U.S. Senate

Soviet Union: a former country that was made up of 15 republics in northern Asia and eastern Europe

State Department: part of the government that deals with relationships with foreign countries

Index